THE TEN: 1–5

—

WRITTEN BY JEFF PRIES

NASHVILLE   DALLAS   MEXICO CITY   RIO DE JANEIRO   BEIJING

Copyright © by Mariner's Impact, 2008

All rights reserved. No portion of this book may be reproduced, stored in a retrieval system, or transmitted in any form or by any means—electronic, mechanical, photocopy, recording, or any other—except for brief quotations in printed reviews, without the prior permission of the publisher.

Published in Nashville, Tennessee. Thomas Nelson is a trademark of Thomas Nelson, Inc.

Published in association with the literary agency of Yates & Yates, LLP, Attorneys and Counselors, Orange, California.

Thomas Nelson, Inc. titles may be purchased in bulk for educational, business, fund-raising, or sales promotional use. For information, please e-mail SpecialMarkets@ThomasNelson.com

All Scripture quotations are taken from the Holy Bible, New Living Translation. Copyright © 1996. Used by permission of Tyndale House Publishers, Inc., Wheaton, Illinois 60189. All rights reserved.

ISBN 978-1-4185-3396-0

Printed in China.
08 09 10 11 12 SS 6 5 4 3 2 1

CONTENTS

Introduction 4

Chapter 1: No Gods, Only Me 8
Chapter 2: Who Do You Worship? 24
Chapter 3: No Wrongful Use of the Lord's Name 40
Chapter 4: Don't Work Your Life Away 56
Chapter 5: Honor Your Father and Mother 72

Leader's Guide 86
Leader's Guide Chapter 1: No Gods, Only Me 91
Leader's Guide Chapter 2: Who Do You Worship? 94
Leader's Guide Chapter 3: No Wrongful Use of the Lord's Name 99
Leader's Guide Chapter 4: Don't Work Your Life Away 103
Leader's Guide Chapter 5: Honor Your Father and Mother 107

■ INTRODUCTION

LIQUID

Five episodes. One story.

God's Word is as true today as it was when it was written.

But for too long, we have looked at God's Word and wondered how it could possibly impact our lives. It's one thing to simply read the Bible. It's something different altogether to understand it. Far too often we read these stories about people in an ancient land, and we're left feeling flat. "What's this got to do with me?" We know in our hearts that what we're reading is true, right, and good, but we can't see any real way to apply it.

That's where *LIQUID* comes in.

LIQUID presents true-to-life stories of characters with real problems. Because what's the point in putting together a study of God's Word that doesn't deal with any of the issues we actually face? Along with each chapter in this book is a film, filled with characters who live in our world—the real world. Yet their problems and struggles mirror the same struggles found in stories in the Bible.

Jesus is the master storyteller. He helped people understand, made them contemplate, made them consider. He wasn't afraid to cut a story a couple of ways, as if he was saying, "Let me say it another way, a different way, so you can understand." He often gave answers by asking questions in return, so people would investigate, think, learn. It's how he did it, so it's why we do it. We translate ancient stories into the language of today's culture, and we ask relevant questions to help you discover the truth for yourself.

Whether you're with a small group, or simply by yourself, all we ask is that you take a deep breath, pop in the DVD, and then read through these pages and think carefully about the questions and the Scriptures. These are not questions from the SAT—they don't have definitive answers. They are designed for you to reflect upon based on your perspective. Everyone's discoveries will be different. But that's what's great about God's truth—it's one truth, but it's formed differently around each person.

It's simply about taking in, reflecting, and coming up with something useful for your life. Now at last we have an immediate, portable, relevant way to experience God's Word. A revolutionary new way to study the Bible.

LIQUID. God's Word flowing through your life.

■ THE TEN: 1–5

Have you ever stopped to consider the other people on the road with you? Their lives, their dreams, what they're dealing with? Think about it—when we're heading down a freeway we may all be traveling in the same direction, but we have so many different motivations driving us.

Most of these drivers haven't thought about the Ten Commandments since they were children. It's been so long, in fact, that they don't even recognize the commandments when they show up in their own lives. But between making idols, remembering the Sabbath, and honoring parents, each driver ends up steering himself down a path that ultimately leads to a choice: will he follow God's road or his own?

The Ten: 1–5 tells the story of five drivers who are faced with just this question. Follow their stories as they choose whether to recognize God's path as more than a set of obsolete stone tablets or to go their own way.

CHAPTER 1: NO GODS, ONLY ME

Do not worship any other gods besides me (Exodus 20:3).

***Worship* is a strong word.** You can admire someone, or you can look up to him, but worship? That's on a whole different level. Not to say I've never done it. I'd have to think back some years, maybe even back to when I was in college and was much more impressionable. As I've gotten older, I am much more hardened, jaded. I see the flaws in people too easily nowadays to actually worship someone. But as a twenty-year-old in college, sure, I worshiped someone. I thought, *If only I could be like him*. Like many guys my age, it was an athlete—Nolan Ryan. The kind of guy who stood on a mound and said, "Here it comes; bet you can't hit it." In my mind, he was a guy who dominated, a guy worth worshiping.

> As you were growing up, who is someone you admired—almost worshiped—and why?

Play video episode now.

Every now and then I'll have a tough day, the kind of day when you let Jesus know "you can come back any time you want, I'm ready." Usually what makes a day tough is when I have to deal with hard-to-deal-with people. They take a toll on me. And as a pastor, people just expect me to be able to take it. But when I get home after one of those days, my wife can usually tell that I need some space. So what I typically do is go out on the front porch by myself, just for some alone time, just to chill out. I'll bet the woman in the film wishes she handled things the same way. Well, I guess, in a way she did.

What were the mistakes the woman in the film made that led to her terrible predicament?

ACTS 17:16–34

¹⁶ While Paul was waiting for them in Athens, he was deeply troubled by all the idols he saw everywhere in the city. ¹⁷ He went to the synagogue to debate with the Jews and the God-fearing Gentiles, and he spoke daily in the public square to all who happened to be there. ¹⁸ He also had a debate with some of the Epicurean and Stoic philosophers. When he told them about Jesus and his resurrection, they said, "This babbler has picked up some strange ideas." Others said, "He's pushing some foreign religion." ¹⁹ Then they took him to the Council of Philosophers. "Come and tell us more about this new religion," they said. ²⁰ "You are saying some rather startling things, and we want to know what it's all about." ²¹(It should be explained that all the Athenians as well as the foreigners in Athens seemed to spend all their time discussing the latest ideas.) ²² So Paul, standing before the Council, addressed them as follows: "Men of Athens, I notice that you are very religious, ²³ for as I was walking along I saw your many altars. And one of them had this inscription on it—'To an Unknown God.' You have been worshiping him without knowing who he is, and now I wish to tell you about him. ²⁴ "He is the God who made the world and everything in it. Since he is Lord of heaven and earth, he doesn't live in man-made temples, ²⁵ and human hands can't serve his needs—for he has no needs. He himself gives life and breath to everything, and he satisfies every need there is. ²⁶ From one man he created all the nations throughout the

whole earth. He decided beforehand which should rise and fall, and he determined their boundaries. ²⁷ "His purpose in all of this was that the nations should seek after God and perhaps feel their way toward him and find him—though he is not far from any one of us. ²⁸ For in him we live and move and exist. As one of your own poets says, 'We are his offspring.' ²⁹ And since this is true, we shouldn't think of God as an idol designed by craftsmen from gold or silver or stone. ³⁰ God overlooked people's former ignorance about these things, but now he commands everyone everywhere to turn away from idols and turn to him. ³¹ For he has set a day for judging the world with justice by the man he has appointed, and he proved to everyone who this is by raising him from the dead." ³² When they heard Paul speak of the resurrection of a person who had been dead, some laughed, but others said, "We want to hear more about this later." ³³ That ended Paul's discussion with them, ³⁴ but some joined him and became believers. Among them were Dionysius, a member of the Council, a woman named Damaris, and others.

What did Paul say about the "unknown God" and why he alone is worthy of worship? How did people respond?

CULTURAL AND HISTORICAL THOUGHTS

At the time Paul entered Athens, the Greeks worshiped as many as thirty thousand gods and goddesses. They were man-made gods but they were taken very seriously. They would erect statues and monuments and altars to these made-up gods. The streets were lined with them; they were in every niche, in every window, and at every doorstep. It has been said that it was easier to find a god than a man. They erected statues, carved idols, and created altars for every god they knew so as not to anger any of them. They were so afraid of angering a god that they erected a statue to "the Unknown God" in case they missed one.

Within the population of Athens there were those who lived two major philosophies: the Epicureans and the Stoics. The Epicureans were consumed with a lifestyle of indulgence, with their main objective in life being pleasure. They believed there was no afterlife and therefore they lived their life in pursuit of pleasures—an "eat, drink, and be merry for tomorrow you die" attitude. The Epicureans believed the gods to be material but thought the gods were too busy being blessed and happy to be bothered with the governance of the universe.

Stoics considered themselves as good as God. God was in everything—rocks, trees, the oceans, birds, every living and non-living thing. The Stoic god is immanent throughout the whole of creation and directed its development down to the smallest detail. Those who lived according to this philosophy tended not to believe anything and were dead to feelings and emotions.

The only thing these two philosophies agreed on was that Paul's teaching was abhorrent to their lifestyle and customs. They considered Paul to be a babbler with no real thought or understanding of his own. Paul spoke of Jesus and a resurrection. The Greek word for "resurrection" is *anastasis* and the word sounded like a female name. It is possible when Paul talked about Jesus and the resurrection in the marketplace, people thought that he was talking about some new god and goddess, Jesus and Anastasis. While Athens was full of religions, a law prohibited the introduction of new foreign gods. So Paul was summoned before the city council to explain himself. This was not a formal trial. There does not seem to be a formal charge, a legal defense, or a verdict. This was most likely an inquiry to determine if laws had been broken.

As I sit and write this, I am out on a ship in the middle of the ocean. All I can see around me is water. No land, no other boats, just water as far as the eye can see. There is an eeriness to it, a great reminder of the vastness of the ocean. It is huge. Waves crash against the ship; the water is powerful. Looking at the size of this huge ocean reminds me of how big God is, how powerful, how vast. The thought that he created everything gets lost in the business and shuffle of life with me. God is big, beyond belief, beyond what can even be imagined, much like the endless miles of ocean. God, like the ocean, is to be respected.

What is worship?

What is it about God that would warrant his being number one?

After reading the responses in the passage, how do you think people respond the same way today?

Every day I am in a tug-of-war with two gods in my life. One God is the creator of all, who loves me and has shown me his love in numerous ways. The other god is more of a love affair, but of a different sort. It's not so much a question of "How do I feel loved by it?" but "How can I love it?" A preoccupation that is filled not so much with what it can do for me, but what I can do for it. The other god? Myself.

Life is a constant tug-of-war between two gods—my Creator and myself. Every day, I need to remind myself to worship God and what he wants, and not focus on myself and what I want. Every day is that great reminder that he is God and I am not!

> What has God done (or is God doing) in your life that makes him worthy of your worship?
>
> What is something specific you can do this week to worship God?

God always wants to be number one in my life. What is my response to God? It depends. Mostly it hinges on where I am in my life and how life is treating me now. There are certainly times when I give God the number-one spot he deserves. Then there are times when I forget and treat him as an afterthought. There are times I have been intrigued by God, wanting to learn so much more about him. Then there are times when I have scoffed at God, not with my lips but with my actions.

I'm trying to learn how to give God the place in my life he deserves, regardless of my circumstance, regardless of how life is operating. Worship God based solely on who he is . . . well, not just who he is, but also because of what he has done!

EXTRA QUESTIONS

What is it about other gods that makes people feel they are "worthy" to be worshiped?

What are three attributes of other "gods" that speak to people?

What are different times in your life when you have responded the same way toward God as the people in the passage?

What keeps you from worshiping God in the way he should be worshiped?

What are ways that you do worship God in a worthy way?

CHAPTER 2: WHO DO YOU WORSHIP?

Do not make idols of any kind, whether in the shape of birds or animals or fish (Exodus 20:4).

***American Idol* is an interesting name.** After all, it is just a singing competition . . . or is it? Isn't it also a great reminder of what we do with people or things? We idolize them, to the degree that thirty million people will call in to support "their idol." I hear stories of people who live or die with their idol's performance; chat rooms are filled with people's responses to their idol's routine. It has become a phenomenon. A little much, perhaps, but remember, we are a society that is entranced by our idols. *American Idol*—do I watch it? Yes, I admit, I'm actually watching it right now and my favorite just finished performing. In fact, I'd better stop writing. I have a call to make.

> What do you like or dislike about the reality TV programs like *American Idol*, *America's Got Talent*, or *America's Best Dance Crew*?

Play video episode now.

What originally seemed like a harmless and even heartwarming relationship took a turn for the worse. What was seen as innocent in the beginning went dark in a hurry. That is what can happen with idols we create. A brief interest can turn into a compulsion, or in some cases even an obsession. Do we ever go to the extent of breaking laws or doing creepy things? Most likely not. But we can take good things in our lives and turn them into obsessions. Do I ever need a restraining order? No. But there are times when I feel like I need to restrain myself.

At what point in the film did you realize that this relationship was not a healthy one?

Put yourself in the shoes of the two main characters. What would you do in their situation?

EXODUS 32:1–24

¹ When Moses failed to come back down the mountain right away, the people went to Aaron. "Look," they said, "make us some gods who can lead us. This man Moses, who brought us here from Egypt, has disappeared. We don't know what has happened to him." ² So Aaron said, "Tell your wives and sons and daughters to take off their gold earrings, and then bring them to me." ³ All the people obeyed Aaron and brought him their gold earrings. ⁴ Then Aaron took the gold, melted it down, and molded and tooled it into the shape of a calf. The people exclaimed, "O Israel, these are the gods who brought you out of Egypt!" ⁵ When Aaron saw how excited the people were about it, he built an altar in front of the calf and announced, "Tomorrow there will be a festival to the Lord!" ⁶ So the people got up early the next morning to sacrifice burnt offerings and peace offerings. After this, they celebrated with feasting and drinking, and indulged themselves in pagan revelry. ⁷ Then the Lord told Moses, "Quick! Go down the mountain! The people you brought from Egypt have defiled themselves. ⁸ They have already turned from the way I commanded them to live. They have made an idol shaped like a calf, and they have worshiped and sacrificed to it. They are saying, 'These are your gods, O Israel, who brought you out of Egypt.'" ⁹ Then the Lord said, "I have seen how stubborn and rebellious these people are. ¹⁰ Now leave me alone so my anger can blaze against them and destroy them all. Then I will make you, Moses, into a great nation instead of them." ¹¹ But Moses pleaded with the Lord his God not to do it. "O Lord!" he exclaimed. "Why are you so angry with your own people whom you brought from the land of Egypt with such great power and mighty acts? ¹² The Egyptians will say, 'God tricked them into coming to the mountains so he could kill them and wipe them from the face of the earth.' Turn away

from your fierce anger. Change your mind about this terrible disaster you are planning against your people! ¹³ Remember your covenant with your servants—Abraham, Isaac, and Jacob. You swore by your own self, 'I will make your descendants as numerous as the stars of heaven. Yes, I will give them all of this land that I have promised to your descendants, and they will possess it forever.'" ¹⁴ So the Lord withdrew his threat and didn't bring against his people the disaster he had threatened. ¹⁵ Then Moses turned and went down the mountain. He held in his hands the two stone tablets inscribed with the terms of the covenant. They were inscribed on both sides, front and back. ¹⁶ These stone tablets were God's work; the words on them were written by God himself. ¹⁷ When Joshua heard the noise of the people shouting below them, he exclaimed to Moses, "It sounds as if there is a war in the camp!" ¹⁸ But Moses replied, "No, it's neither a cry of victory nor a cry of defeat. It is the sound of a celebration." ¹⁹ When they came near the camp, Moses saw the calf and the dancing. In terrible anger, he threw the stone tablets to the ground, smashing them at the foot of the mountain. ²⁰ He took the calf they had made and melted it in the fire. And when the metal had cooled, he ground it into powder and mixed it with water. Then he made the people drink it. ²¹ After that, he turned to Aaron. "What did the people do to you?" he demanded. "How did they ever make you bring such terrible sin upon them?" ²²"Don't get upset, sir," Aaron replied. "You yourself know these people and what a wicked bunch they are. ²³ They said to me, 'Make us some gods to lead us, for something has happened to this man Moses, who led us out of Egypt.' ²⁴ So I told them, 'Bring me your gold earrings.' When they brought them to me, I threw them into the fire—and out came this calf!"

What led Aaron to create an idol? What was the idol, and what was it supposed to provide?

What was the reaction to the idol by the people? Aaron? God? Moses?

CULTURAL AND HISTORICAL THOUGHTS

Moses was on Mount Sinai encapsulated by the cloud of glory that was the presence of the Lord. The Israelites were encamped below the summit of the mountain. The cloud appeared as consuming fire to the Israelites below.

The Israelites had recently been set free from four hundred years of slavery in Egypt. In the past few weeks the Israelites had witnessed miracles and provision from God, such as daily quail and manna from heaven, his guidance from a pillar of clouds by day and a pillar of fire by night, the parting of the Red Sea to allow dry passage, water springing from a rock, bitter water turned sweet, and salvation from the pursuing Egyptians.

Moses had previously gone to the summit of Mount Sinai, which was consumed by the presence of the Lord, to receive the commandments for his people. In addition, Aaron and Nadab, Abihu, and the seventy elders of Israel had been on the mountain and saw the presence of the Lord. At this particular time, Moses and Joshua had gone to the summit of the mountain to receive more instructions from God. Moses was gone for forty days and forty nights.

The night before Moses returned, the people got anxious waiting for him to come back. Even though they were being provided for, they got nervous and impatient and felt a need to have a tangible god to worship and praise.

Aaron, the brother of Moses, was left in charge while Moses was away. He had been present when Moses brought the commandments down from the mountain previously and was well aware of the second commandment, which stated, "Do not make idols of any kind, whether in the shape of birds or animals or fish. You must never worship or bow down to them, for I, the Lord your God, am a jealous God who will not share your affection with any other god!" (Exodus 20:4–5).

My kids want me to get a new car. They see a Lamborghini and tell me, "That should be your next car, Dad." Fat chance. But I do have my eye on a new car . . . not that I would actually get it, but I have my eye on it. A black Chevy Tahoe. We all have that one car—the dream we would love to have and some of us could maybe even afford if we wanted to treat ourselves. The problem is, when you start to think about a car and really have that "should I get one?" moment, what starts happening? You begin to see it everywhere. Every turn, every light, there it is. You start fixating on it, maybe even obsessing over it. Do I idolize the Chevy Tahoe? No, I'm not that obsessed . . . not until I get behind the wheel.

What leads people to create idols today?

What are idols you see people creating, and what are they supposed to provide?

One of the things I love to do most in life is play golf. I know, it doesn't sound too spiritual or family oriented, but I have been bitten by the golf bug. I will often get invited from someone in the church to play at the local country club. It's a beautiful course that makes me feel like I'm out in the middle of nowhere. When I drive up, someone greets me, carries my clubs, and refers to me as Mr. Pries (of course I always turn around, thinking my dad is standing behind me). I play a great round of golf on a beautifully manicured course, and when I'm done they clean my clubs and even want to carry them to my car for me. But since I'm embarrassed by my car, I carry my clubs myself. When I climb in my car, though, I'm always thinking, *I could get used to this.* Wow, what a day, what a life. The guy who belongs to that club, he's my idol.

> What idols have you created in your life? Have they performed as you expected?
>
> How will you destroy these idols, and what will you replace them with?

My senior year in high school was a magical year for me in sports. I played on some great teams and won championships in both baseball and basketball. It was one of those incredible years when everything I did just worked. It was a year filled with honor after honor, trophy after trophy. In fact, my folks took the trophies and filled up an entire wall that we jokingly named "The Wall of Fame." I didn't think much of it then because I knew it was my folks just being proud of me, but now I feel a little embarrassed as I think of that wall. I hope people weren't turned off by the fact that we had it in the house. We were just celebrating a fun year for the family, but it could have looked different. It could have looked like I was setting up little idols of myself. Wow, I cringe at the thought. I saw the trophies last month in my folks' attic, filled with dust and cobwebs, just lying in a pile. It took me back to those great years, but it also reminded me that so many things in life come and go and what really matters is to hold on to something that lasts.

EXTRA QUESTIONS

What is it that makes people idolize things in their lives?

When does admiration cross the line to idolatry?

What makes us at times give up on having God as our idol?

CHAPTER 3: NO WRONGFUL USE OF THE LORD'S NAME

Do not misuse the name of the LORD your God (Exodus 20:7).

Nicknames can be flattering, or even fun. Take Willie Mays, the "Say Hey Kid," or Frank Sinatra, "Ol' Blue Eyes." Okay, I'm dating myself with these examples. But nicknames have been around forever. The only one I have ever gotten was as a kid. It wasn't too flattering, so I'm really glad it didn't stick. "Jeffrey Giraffe." I know, now you know why it didn't stick. Can you guess why people gave me that name? Yeah, I may have been a little tall for my age. We have all gotten a nickname at one time or another. If I can share mine, anyone can.

What's the story behind your name or nickname?

Play video episode now.

Bottled water is a national craze. But for twenty years I did the unthinkable, the unimaginable: I drank water out of the tap. And as a kid I actually used to drink it out of the hose! Can you believe it? And I'm still alive! For some reason, though, now I only drink bottled water. It's probably because I'm lazy. I can take it with me anywhere. Do I have a favorite brand of water? Sure, but usually I just buy the cheapest option. You don't have to work too hard to sell water; just bottle it. Something you probably shouldn't do is use God's name to sell water. Sure, you might sell a little water, but you might lose a whole lot more.

How does the salesman in the film use God's name in a way it was not intended?

Is there a way he could have sold his product without leveraging God's name inappropriately?

MARK 11:14–17

¹⁴ Then Jesus said to the tree, "May no one ever eat your fruit again!" And the disciples heard him say it. ¹⁵ When they arrived back in Jerusalem, Jesus entered the Temple and began to drive out the merchants and their customers. He knocked over the tables of the money changers and the stalls of those selling doves, ¹⁶ and he stopped everyone from bringing in merchandise. ¹⁷ He taught them, "The Scriptures declare, 'My Temple will be called a place of prayer for all nations,' but you have turned it into a den of thieves."

JOHN 2:14–16

¹⁴ In the Temple area he saw merchants selling cattle, sheep, and doves for sacrifices; and he saw money changers behind their counters. ¹⁵ Jesus made a whip from some ropes and chased them all out of the Temple. He drove out the sheep and oxen, scattered the money changers' coins over the floor, and turned over their tables. ¹⁶ Then, going over to the people who sold doves, he told them, "Get these things out of here. Don't turn my Father's house into a marketplace!"

What were the people in the Temple doing, and what was Jesus' response?

CULTURAL AND HISTORICAL THOUGHTS

The Jewish Temple was a magnificent structure. It soared almost fifteen stories above the Kidron Valley floor to the east. It was nearly five hundred yards long and four hundred yards wide. The outer court of the Temple compound was nearly the size of fifteen football fields.

The purpose of the businesses within the Temple grounds was legitimate and legal and provided a needed service. Faithful Jews were expected to offer animal sacrifices and financial gifts at the Temple. Oftentimes pilgrims who had traveled from afar found it more convenient to buy their animals in Jerusalem rather than transport them across the country.

Jesus entered the Temple grounds on the Monday of the last week of his life on earth. His triumphant entry into Jerusalem had taken place three days earlier, and he knew his betrayal, trial, and death were imminent.

When Jesus entered the Temple grounds, pens of sheep, goats, doves, and other sacrificial animals were everywhere. Money changers operated other tables. The priests and/or other local politicians maintained strict control over the franchises for these Temple businesses, often demanding a kickback. Once a limited number of merchants had a corner on the market, they were free to conduct business as they pleased. The money changers would charge exorbitant fees and the animal sellers would mark up their prices.

The priests had a system to take care of any competing markets that might crop up outside the Temple grounds. Before an animal could be sacrificed, it had to pass a Temple inspection. The priests who were getting a kickback would simply reject any animal that didn't come from their licensed merchants. The whole system was filled with greed and corruption.

I think we have all seen those religious figures on TV asking for money. Are all of them bad? Of course not. A lot of good is done by the work of pastors and ministries on TV or on the radio. But my brain does tend to automatically assume that they have self-serving motivations. It's probably because of the "one bad apple" concept. I hear about one guy who is crying out for money on television while he lives in some ten-thousand-square-foot house and drives an eighty-thousand-dollar Mercedes, and it ruins the reputation for all the other TV evangelists. Taking God's name and using it in a way he doesn't intend for it to be used does more than bring God to tears. It makes him angry.

When do you see people do things in the "name of God," yet you know that what they are doing is not motivated by God?

What are reasons that people use or leverage the name of God?

What can people do to bring their actions more in alignment with what God really wants and make it less about what they want?

There are real subtleties to the idea of using God's name in a way that is inappropriate, or not in his will. As a pastor, I have to be very careful with this because so much of what I do is perceived as something that God is supporting. And people certainly feel like when they bless me, they are blessing God. As a pastor you can leverage your position in a way that is inappropriate. I usually have to filter my actions through the idea of: does it honor God or is it dishonoring to God? And as always, the real question is: what are my motives? If my motives aren't pure, I don't do it. That is a good filter for everything we do. Is it dishonoring to God? Are our motives pure?

When have you done something in the name of God, yet it had nothing to do with God? How did it make you feel?

Where in your life are you, even in the most subtle way, using God's name for personal gain instead of God's glory?

How would your life be different if your motivation was solely to honor God instead of yourself? What would you need to change? What would the results look like?

I became a Christian in high school. I went to youth group all the time, not as one of the first-row guys, but mostly as one of the cool guys who sat in the back and leaned his chair against the wall. But my faith in God was important to me. On my basketball team there was a guy who took the Lord's name in vain constantly. I didn't know what to do. I could get in his face and ask him to lay off, but I was pretty sure that would only upset him. I asked my youth pastor and he told me to use the line "Don't blame God." I don't know if it was the best line to use; I don't know if it even worked. Heck, I probably mumbled it so softly he didn't even hear, but at least I did something. Hearing those words bugged me, and I'm pretty sure they bugged God. When do you take a stand?

EXTRA QUESTIONS

Where do you feel the line is drawn between what is appropriate use and inappropriate use of God's name?

What is your response when you hear people take the Lord's name in vain? Does your response work or not? If you yourself struggle with this, what can you do to stop?

CHAPTER 4: DON'T WORK YOUR LIFE AWAY

Remember to observe the Sabbath day by keeping it holy (Exodus 20:8).

I just got back from a vacation—a three-day cruise to Mexico with our friends. Never again. It wasn't the people; it just didn't feel like much of a vacation. You see, I hate boats. A cruise for a guy who hates boats is like a guy who hates flying trying to become a pilot, or a person who doesn't want responsibility deciding to have kids. The two just don't go together. You know it's going to be a tough vacation when from the moment it starts you can't wait for it to be over. The bright side is that I am now home in my own bed, in my house. The bad news—one week later I still feel like I'm on a boat. It's the vacation that never ends. Normally that's a good thing, but in this case, I'll pass.

Where did you go on your last vacation?

Play video episode now.

If only I had the ability to do something over again. To be more attentive, be in the moment, take time to be with someone. We all have those moments in life when we say, "If I could only do it again, I'd do it this way." As I watch this episode, I can see myself as the main character. There are a series of *A Christmas Carol* moments—chances to get a glimpse of how I acted and what the results have been. It's that great reminder to slow down, that things can wait. Do I expect to live life with no regrets? Of course not. But I can live with less regret. Usually when I slow down and take my time, take that extra moment, my life plays out better. It's a pretty simple equation: taking more time and doing less equals fewer regrets.

From the perspective of the father, the mother, and the boy, what might have each character been feeling during the flashbacks?

What does the film say to you?

GENESIS 1

¹ In the beginning God created the heavens and the earth. ² The earth was empty, a formless mass cloaked in darkness. And the Spirit of God was hovering over its surface. ³ Then God said, "Let there be light," and there was light. ⁴ And God saw that it was good. Then he separated the light from the darkness. ⁵ God called the light "day" and the darkness "night." Together these made up one day. ⁶ And God said, "Let there be space between the waters, to separate water from water." ⁷ And so it was. God made this space to separate the waters above from the waters below. ⁸ And God called the space "sky." This happened on the second day. ⁹ And God said, "Let the waters beneath the sky be gathered into one place so dry ground may appear." And so it was. ¹⁰ God named the dry ground "land" and the water "seas." And God saw that it was good. ¹¹ Then God said, "Let the land burst forth with every sort of grass and seed-bearing plant. And let there be trees that grow seed-bearing fruit. The seeds will then produce the kinds of plants and trees from which they came." And so it was. ¹² The land was filled with seed-bearing plants and trees, and their seeds produced plants and trees of like kind. And God saw that it was good. ¹³ This all happened on the third day. ¹⁴ And God said, "Let bright lights appear in the sky to separate the day from the night. They will be signs to mark off the seasons, the days, and the years. ¹⁵ Let their light shine down upon the earth." And so it was. ¹⁶ For God made two great lights, the sun and the moon, to shine down upon the earth. The greater one, the sun, presides during the day; the lesser one, the moon,

presides through the night. He also made the stars. [17] God set these lights in the heavens to light the earth, [18] to govern the day and the night, and to separate the light from the darkness. And God saw that it was good. [19] This all happened on the fourth day. [20] And God said, "Let the waters swarm with fish and other life. Let the skies be filled with birds of every kind." [21] So God created great sea creatures and every sort of fish and every kind of bird. And God saw that it was good. [22] Then God blessed them, saying, "Let the fish multiply and fill the oceans. Let the birds increase and fill the earth." [23] This all happened on the fifth day. [24] And God said, "Let the earth bring forth every kind of animal—livestock, small animals, and wildlife." And so it was. [25] God made all sorts of wild animals, livestock, and small animals, each able to reproduce more of its own kind. And God saw that it was good. [26] Then God said, "Let us make people in our image, to be like ourselves. They will be masters over all life—the fish in the sea, the birds in the sky, and all the livestock, wild animals, and small animals." [27] So God created people in his own image; God patterned them after himself; male and female he created them. [28] God blessed them and told them, "Multiply and fill the earth and subdue it. Be masters over the fish and birds and all the animals." [29] And God said, "Look! I have given you the seed-bearing plants throughout the earth and all the fruit trees for your food. [30] And I have given all the grasses and other green plants to the animals and birds for their food." And so it was. [31] Then God looked over all he had made, and he saw that it was excellent in every way. This all happened on the sixth day.

GENESIS 2:1–4

¹ So the creation of the heavens and the earth and everything in them was completed. ² On the seventh day, having finished his task, God rested from all his work. ³ And God blessed the seventh day and declared it holy, because it was the day when he rested from his work of creation. ⁴ This is the account of the creation of the heavens and the earth.

What did God do in each of the six days? What did he rest from on the seventh day?

CULTURAL AND HISTORICAL THOUGHTS

The term "Sabbath" comes from the Hebrew verb *shabbat*, which means primarily "to cease." A second meaning is "to rest." God rested on the seventh day from all of his work, so we, who were created in his image, should also lay down our work and rest on the seventh day. The Israelites understood this and they observed the Sabbath with a special celebration. The fourth commandment was extended to not only the Israelites but also the entire family, the servants, and even the animals.

The Sabbath is a time to abstain completely from everyday work. It is a time to relax mind, body, and soul in order to be filled, nourished, and freed from the worry and anxiety that goes along with everyday life. The Sabbath is not designed as a time to run away from life and its problems; rather it is an opportunity to receive grace to face them. It is a chance to refocus and put God back in the center of one's life, and an opportunity to connect with people and deepen relationships.

Is a week only seven days? It feels so much longer than that, more like twelve days. Maybe it's just that I try to squeeze twelve days into seven. How do I fill my week? Maybe the more proper term is *overfill*. With four kids—who are all in sports—a job, and a wife, I have no life. I don't live; I survive. My guess is that this situation isn't unique to me. I'll bet you feel the same way.

What are some different ways in which people fill up their seven days each week?

Last night my two young daughters asked if they could sit down and read to me. This is when TiVo really comes in handy. I paused the Lakers game and sat down to read with my daughters. As I was sitting there, I was thinking, *There is no greater moment, just alone on the couch giving my undivided attention to my two little readers.* There was something special about the solitude, the quietness. Sure, I am with my girls all the time, but seldom like this: quiet, listening, connecting, giving them a sense that I really care. I need to do that more with my girls. It made me think of God and how I am with him during the day—either in some panic-stricken moment crying out to him, or in some jam asking him for help. But seldom am I quiet with him, seldom do I "pause life" and just settle in with God, listening, taking time, connecting in a special way. I fight for those moments with my daughters. I'm thinking I need to fight more for those moments with my God.

What are all of the things you do in a typical week?

What would it look like to spend one out of every seven days either resting or taking a break from work?

The Sabbath can "just be a day of rest." How does this view of the Sabbath differ from your previous thoughts?

Busyness is doing: to be productive you have to be on the go, making things happen. If I can accomplish three things during the day, there is nothing that should keep me from accomplishing four or five. The more I do, the better I am and the further I'm getting. The more I accomplish, the more valuable I become— in my work, with my family. The thought of stopping, slowing down, just feels like such a waste. If I'm reading, I'm not working. If I'm resting, I'm wasting time.

I make the mistake of thinking the more I do makes a better me. When my life is out of balance, overwhelming, and slightly out of control, that is me at my worst. I need to stop, take time, and rejuvenate. Resting, slowing down, and finding solitude with God makes me *ME* at my best. Slowing down to do more and be more effective—wow, that's a foreign concept, yet deep down I know it makes a better me.

EXTRA QUESTIONS

What is it that keeps people from slowing down in general?

What is it that keeps people from slowing down and spending time with God?

What keeps you from slowing down in life and with God?

Slowing down often means saying no to things. What are things in your life you should say no to in order to have more time to do the things you need to do?

CHAPTER 5: HONOR YOUR FATHER AND MOTHER

Honor your father and mother. Then you will live a long, full life in the land the L<small>ORD</small> your God will give you (Exodus 20:12).

Growing up there seemed to be a lot of rules in my family. Most of them, however, were kind of understood. My brother and I knew we just had to do what was right because our dad was strict. The good news was we weren't overly rebellious kids so we both wanted to do the right thing. The one rule that I remember the most was "You don't leave the dinner table until all of your food has been eaten." It's a pretty simple rule, actually. I guess it taught me a couple of things that I still hold on to: the need to eat fast, and eat everything in sight! Who says our parents' rules are crazy?

> As a kid, what were some rules you had to obey that you thought were crazy or you just didn't like?

Play video episode now.

We've all had second chances. It doesn't matter how old you are; we all need them. Second chances are hard to get, and they're even harder to give. Even to someone as close to you as your mom, giving that second chance can be a challenge, especially when you feel she has been letting you down for an entire lifetime. Forgiving someone is one thing, but actually holding them up and honoring them takes it to a whole new level. You want to have a real party, one that is worth celebrating? Try learning to find the good in your parents when you don't think it's possible—enough good that can actually lead you to giving them a place of honor. Blow out the candles; there's a party going on.

How is your family like / not like the family in the film?

What makes honoring the grandmother easy?

What makes it difficult?

EPHESIANS 6:1–3

¹ Children, obey your parents because you belong to the Lord, for this is the right thing to do. ² "Honor your father and mother." This is the first of the Ten Commandments that ends with a promise. ³ And this is the promise: If you honor your father and mother, "you will live a long life, full of blessing."

PROVERBS 23:22–25

²² Listen to your father, who gave you life, and don't despise your mother's experience when she is old. ²³ Get the truth and don't ever sell it; also get wisdom, discipline, and discernment. ²⁴ The father of godly children has cause for joy. What a pleasure it is to have wise children. ²⁵ So give your parents joy! May she who gave you birth be happy.

What do you learn from these passages about the parent/child relationship?

CULTURAL AND HISTORICAL THOUGHTS

The Hebrew word for "honor," *kah-bed*, means "to give weight to or make weighty with respect." The link between "heavy" and "honor" is understood against the background of the ancient world, in which a heavy person was obviously affluent and thereby honored; so the verse could be translated: "Respect your father and your mother." Within the Jewish family structure from Old Testament times until today, there has always been a sense of order and identity that gave them strength, perspective, and discipline. At the heart of the family structure was a reverence for parents, a high regard, a respect, and an esteem for the older members of the family.

The word Paul uses for "children" in Ephesians is *teknia* and it doesn't mean little ones, but refers to any person living under the roof of a parent's home. It is not about age; it is about position. By honoring our parents, we are honoring God. Respect for parents is a pivotal point of faith in the entire Bible.

In the fifth commandment, to "honor" means to commit oneself to elevating his or her parents' status by providing them with a comfortable life, such as taking care of needs and welfare. Children must refrain from doing anything that might cause their parents to be disgraced or disregarded. God reveres this principle of honoring parents so much that it is the only commandment in the Ten Commandments to offer a promise of reward for those who accept and follow it.

My favorite movie of all time is *A Few Good Men*. I like it for many reasons, partly because I love good courtroom drama. But I mostly love it because it is a movie about honor. It's about taking a principle and holding it up and saying, "This is how I'm going to be," even if it means I end up in jail. The two marines in the movie didn't just talk about it; they didn't just see it in the lives around them—they lived it. They lived by a code. They lived with respect. It was a value that they were willing to not just live for but die for. Now that is honor.

What does *honor* mean? What doesn't it mean?

What are ways to honor parents at different stages of life (as a child, teenager, young adult, and adult, and as parents become elderly and pass away)?

Today is my mom's seventieth birthday. There is not a more wonderful woman in the whole world than my mom. I didn't realize this as much when I was young. Back then she was just Mom to me. But now that I look back at her life, I realize she is an amazing woman. As a kid, I honored her because my dad would come down on me if I didn't. As I grew up and matured, I honored her because she was always there for me, and I couldn't help but honor her. But in my younger years, honoring Mom just meant obeying her. Now that she is older, honoring has taken on a different meaning. What does she want now? She just wants to know that I will be there for her. Honoring Mom and Dad—it may look different to you as time passes, but it is always important.

> What are ways you've shown honor to your parents? How can you honor them at this point in your life? What about in the future?

I'm sitting by a pool with my friend as we watch our children play and swim. I asked him if his folks were still alive, because I had never heard him talk about his parents. He said his dad left him when he was three months old, that he had never known his father. He looks at his children and says, "Being a parent, I don't know how someone could just leave their child." He said he would like to someday track down his dad and confront him, and maybe not in a nice way. Honoring parents—it's not always easy to do, or even to talk about.

EXTRA QUESTIONS

When you were growing up, what made it hard to honor your parents? In your life today, what makes it hard to honor your parents?

What is the greatest thrill about showing honor to your parents?

If you are a parent, what would it feel like to be honored? Knowing what you know now, how do you honor your parents differently? Or how do you wish you had honored your parents differently?

LEADER'S GUIDE

THE TEN: 1–5 | 86

■ NOTE TO LEADERS

As leaders, we have tried to make this experience as easy for you as possible. Don't try to do too much during your time together as a group—just ask and listen, and direct when necessary.

The questions have a flow, a progression, and are designed to get people talking. If you help the group start talking early on, they will continue to talk. You will notice that the questions start out easy and casual, creating a theme. The theme continues throughout the session, flowing through casual topics, then into world affairs, and then they begin getting personal.

When the questions ask about the Bible, spend time there. Dig in and scour the passage. Keep looking. You and your group will discover that looking into the Bible can be fun and interesting. Maybe you already know that, but there will be people in your group who don't—people who are afraid of their Bibles, or who don't think they can really study them.

Remember, we are seeking life change. This will happen by taking God's Word and applying it to your life, and to the lives of the people you are with. That's the goal for each person in the group. Fight for it.

▰ TIPS

So, are you a little nervous? Guess what—I get scared too. I always have a little apprehension when it comes to leading a group. It's what keeps me on my toes! Here are some things to keep in mind as you're preparing.

Think about your group. How does this week's topic relate to your group? Is this going to be an easy session? Is this going to be a challenge? The more at ease you are with the topic, the better the experience will be for your group.

Go over the leader's material early, and try to get to know the questions. Sometimes there are multiple questions provided at the end of the chapters. These are extra questions that can be used as supplemental questions at any point throughout the discussion. Look over these extra questions and see if any of them jump out at you. Don't feel that you have to address each question, but they are there if you need them. My worst nightmare is to be leading a group, and, with thirty minutes still left on the clock, we run out of questions and there's nothing left to talk about . . . so we sit there and stare at one another in painful silence.

Just remember to keep moving through all the questions. The most important goal of this study is to get personal and see how to apply biblical truths to your own life. When you're talking about how a passage plays out in the world today, a common mistake is to not take it deep enough . . . not to push the envelope and move it from what "they" should do to what "I" should do. As a leader, you will struggle with how much to push, how deep to dig. Sometimes it will be just right, sometimes you will push too hard, or sometimes not hard enough. Though it can be nerve-racking, it's the essence of being a leader.

Here are a few more tips:

- Get them talking, laughing, and having fun.
- Don't squelch emotion. Though it may tend to make you uncomfortable, to the point where you'll want to step in and rescue the moment, remember that leaders shouldn't always interfere.
- Jump in when needed. If the question is tough, make sure to model the answer. Try to be open about your own life. Often, the group will only go as deep as you are willing to go.
- When you look in the Bible for answers, don't quit too soon. Let people really search.
- Don't be afraid of silence.
- Lead the group—don't dominate it.

These are just a few things to think about before you begin.

CHAPTER 1: NO GODS, ONLY ME

As you were growing up, who is someone you admired—almost worshiped—and why?

Leader note: Most people had someone in their life whom they admired almost to the point of worshiping them. It could be a sports star, a movie star, or even a personal friend, teacher, or mentor. People have a tendency to worship other people for attributes they wish they possessed. If you wanted to be a football quarterback, you might worship Bret Favre, or earlier greats like Joe Montana or Joe Theismann. If you wanted to be a singer, you might have worshiped the Beatles. Maybe you are the adventurous type and worshiped Evel Knievel or the astronauts who walked on the moon.

What were the mistakes the woman in the film made that led to her terrible predicament?

Leader tip: Use this time to have a discussion on how the woman in the film took things into her own hands. She wanted to play God while also blackmailing the doctor to do what she wanted. Remember, it is good to discuss the film but don't spend too much time in this area. Save a majority of your time to discuss the Bible passage.

Read Acts 17:16–34. What did Paul say about the "unknown God" and why he alone is worthy of worship? How did people respond?

Paul's Message:
• He is the God who made the world and everything in it. • Since he is Lord of heaven and earth, he doesn't live in man-made temples. • Human hands can't serve his needs—for he has no needs. • He himself gives life and breath to everything, and he satisfies every need. • From one man he created all the nations throughout the whole earth. • He decided beforehand when they should rise and fall, and he determined their boundaries. • His purpose was for the nations to seek after God and perhaps feel their way toward him and find him. • He is not far from any one of us. • For in him we live and move and exist. • We are his offspring. • We shouldn't think of God as an idol designed by craftsmen from gold or silver or stone. • He overlooked people's ignorance about these things in earlier times. • He commands everyone everywhere to repent of their sins and turn to him. • He has set a day for judging the world with justice by the man he has appointed. • He proved to everyone who this is by raising him from the dead.

People's Response:
• Some laughed in contempt. • Others said, "We want to hear more about this later." • Some joined him and became believers.

What is worship? What is it about God that would warrant his being number one? After reading the responses in the passage, how do you think people respond the same way today?

Leader tip: Let your group define *worship* on their own first, but then you might want to look up *worship* or have synonyms and the definition printed out for your group and read it together. Some synonyms for *worship* are: *adore*, *love*, *revere*, *respect*, *devote*, *pray to*, *deify*, *adulate*, *venerate*. The definition from the *Encarta* dictionary for *worship* is: "treat somebody or something as deity, as divine and show respect by engaging in acts of prayer and devotion."

Leader tip: Go through each statement you wrote in the observation questions and ask, "Why would you worship God for that?" For instance, "He is the God who made the world and everything in it." You would worship God for that because no one else is able to create life and matter. "He satisfies every need" is praiseworthy because he is the provider and he is faithful. Continue through the rest of the observations in the same way.

What has God done (or is God doing) in your life that makes him worthy of your worship? What is something specific you can do this week to worship God?

Leader tip: It is good to remember God's work in our lives in the past, but if a group member focuses on an example from a long time ago, you may want to also ask for a more current example. It is always good to be aware of how God is working in our lives today.

Leader tip: For the second part of this question, have your group consider different ways they can worship God this week. Some ways to worship are taking time to study his Word, praying in a quiet place where you can be alone, journaling and listing the attributes of God and why you are thankful to him, attending weekly church services, and serving your community.

CHAPTER 2: WHO DO YOU WORSHIP?

> What do you like or dislike about the reality TV programs like *American Idol*, *America's Got Talent*, or *America's Best Dance Crew*?

Leader tip: People either love or hate these types of shows. Some see it as a way to give a chance to people who otherwise might never get one, while others see it as a way to sensationalize lack of talent, or even just as a waste of time. This should create a good, healthy discussion within your group. Just remind them there is no real right or wrong way to feel; it is just personal opinion. The purpose of this question is for your group to grasp the idea that idols, or heroes, can be created and even heralded as praiseworthy for little more than God-given talent.

> At what point in the film did you realize that this relationship was not a healthy one? Put yourself in the shoes of the two main characters. What would you do in their situation?

Leader tip: At some point the story turns, and you begin to realize this relationship isn't a healthy one. Create a discussion around when it turns, and then talk about how different people might handle things differently. Remember, don't spend too much of your time here; save it instead for talking about the Bible and its application in peoples' lives.

▌Read Exodus 32:1–24. What led Aaron to create an idol? What was the idol, and what was it supposed to provide?

Leader tip: This is a long passage, so it's a good idea to read the question first and then read the passage so your group can be considering the answers as you read.

- The people were tired of waiting for Moses to come back from the mountain. • They started doubting Moses (calling him that fellow who brought them out of Egypt). • They asked Aaron to make them some gods that could lead them. • He created a god in the shape of a calf with melted gold given by the people. • They were looking for something to worship and they immediately worshiped the golden calf.

▌What was the reaction to the idol by the people? Aaron? God? Moses?

Leader tip: You might want to have a large piece of paper or whiteboard on which you can list the reactions for each person.

The People:
- They worshiped the calf, proclaiming its greatness: They exclaimed, *"These are your gods, O Israel, who brought you out of Egypt."* • They sacrificed burnt offerings and peace offerings. • They celebrated with feasting and drinking. • They indulged in pagan revelry.

Aaron:
- Once he saw the people's delight in the idol, he created an altar for it. • He proclaimed, "Tomorrow there will be a festival to the Lord!" for the idol. • He blamed the "evil" people and said that all he did was throw the gold in the fire and out came the calf.

God:
- He sent Moses down the mountain to the people. • He told Moses the people had corrupted themselves. • He said the people turned away from his commands. • He told Moses to leave him alone in his fierce anger so he could destroy Israel but that he would not destroy Moses, but instead make him into a great nation. • He changed his mind after Moses' pleading.

Moses:
- He tried to pacify God by telling him his true power would not be shown if Israel was destroyed. • He pleaded with God to change his mind about destroying them, reminding him of Abraham, Isaac, and Jacob and his oath to make them a great nation. • He went down the mountain with the two stone tablets inscribed by God himself. • He was furious when he saw the people worshiping the calf. • He threw the stone tablets to the ground, smashing

them at the foot of the mountain. • He took the calf they had made and burned it. Then he ground it into powder, threw it into the water, and forced the people to drink it. • He asked Aaron to explain what the people could have done to make him create the idol.

■ What leads people to create idols today? What are idols you see people creating, and what are they supposed to provide?

Leader tip: What you want your group to realize is that everyone creates idols of some sort. It may not feel like they are creating a "god" or something to worship, but in reality everyone creates something in their life to give it meaning when they are searching or feeling abandoned or isolated. People create idols when they want to feel powerful or, at the very least, sufficient. They may not "think" it is an idol since they didn't manually form something, set it on an altar, and bow down to it. It could be a person, a job, a bank account, a relationship, an addiction, or something that pacifies them and serves a purpose in their life.

■ What idols have you created in your life? Have they performed as you expected?

Leader tip: Someone in your group may have built up a big bank account to provide security. They may be watching it being destroyed right now due to the economy or other setbacks or downturns. Their idol they had as security is now most likely their biggest worry or insecurity. The same can be true if someone makes their marriage their idol. Cracks and breaks in relationships with their spouses can cause their idol to become weak and ineffective, giving them a sense of failure and inadequacy. Maybe it is their health, and now they are worried about a prognosis or symptom they have.

■ **How will you destroy those idols, and what will you replace them with?**

Leader tip: It can take determination and outright anger to bring down an idol and the associated worship that goes along with it. Have your group consider how they will get angry or emotional enough to destroy whatever bondage has been created by their idols. Explore how a healthy relationship with God can replace each and every idol they've created. What attribute of God will fill the need that pushed them to create the idol in the first place? If it is a bank account, replace it with the promise of God's provision. If it is the fear of being alone or abandonment that led to a marriage being an idol, rest in God's promise that he will never leave you or forsake you and that he loves you.

Leader tip: If you have a group member who talks about an addiction or anything that requires follow-up after your group meets, be sure to seek the proper counsel for that person. Help be accountable for their ongoing care.

■ CHAPTER 3: NO WRONGFUL USE OF THE LORD'S NAME

■ What's the story behind your name or nickname?

Leader tip: This should be an easy question for your group to answer. Your group can talk about how their parents chose their first name, or how they received a unique nickname.

How does the salesman in the film use God's name in a way it was not intended? Is there a way he could have sold his product without leveraging God's name inappropriately?

Leader tip: The salesman's motivation was not to point people to God, but only to make money. He could have still sold the water by using his creativity to come up with an advertising campaign that didn't use God's name in vain. As always, watch your time, because there are a lot of questions in this session.

Read Mark 11:14–17 and John 2:14–16. What were the people in the Temple doing, and what was Jesus' response?

The People:
• They were buying and selling animals (cattle, sheep, and doves). • They were buying and selling the animals to offer for sacrifices. • There were money changers and dealers exchanging foreign currency. • They were using the Temple as a marketplace.

Jesus' Response:
• He was angry. • He made a whip from rope. • He drove out the people. • He stopped everyone from using the Temple as a marketplace. • He chased the dealers out. • He knocked over the tables of the money changers. • He drove out the livestock. • He told the people selling doves to get them out of there. • He scattered the money all over the floor. • He quoted Scripture saying, "*'My Temple will be called a place of prayer for all nations,' but you have turned it into a den of thieves*." • He reminded everyone this was the Father's house and was to be kept holy and used only for those things of God—not making money.

When do you see people do things in the "name of God," yet you know that what they are doing is not motivated by God?

Leader tip: Have your group consider people they know who go to church with motives other than worshiping or growing in their faith. There are those who go to network and to put on appearances. There are those who serve only to be seen serving or only for something nice to put on a résumé.

What are reasons that people use or leverage the name of God?

Leader tip: There would be a lot of reasons for people to use the name of God in their work and endeavors—first of all, the name of God carries a lot of weight in most circles. Motives seem pure and noble when associated with the name of God. Sometimes people use the name of God to set a tone for what they are seeking. Most often, when people use the name of God for personal gain, their motivation is complete selfishness.

What can people do to bring their actions more in alignment with what God really wants and make it less about what they want?

Leader tip: The first thing people need to do is recognize that what they are doing is not right; then they can begin to address their actions and tweak them to be more in line with God's will. For instance, if someone is doing service work for the mere benefit of what it will do for a college application, they can step back from that particular activity and consider what they really want the end result to be. If they are passionate about the cause, they simply have to focus more on the cause and less on their personal gain. But there are other more serious situations that go deeper than just a change in focus—a change of heart is really what is needed.

When have you done something in the name of God, yet it had nothing to do with God? How did it make you feel?

Leader tip: As a leader you may want to be the first to answer this question, as it can be a bit painful to answer. There may be guilty feelings or regret as people share, so be prepared for an emotional response.

Leader tip: Have your group consider even the most subtle personal gain they got from doing something for the church, such as when they were in youth group to meet that cute boy or girl, or when they went on a missions trip because it was somewhere they always wanted to see, or going to the men's breakfast to be with that business contact they haven't been able to get time with. Maybe you got free registration for your kids if you volunteered for VBS and you chose the position with the very least time and effort. In this situation, the focus was not on helping the ministry, but rather the free admission. How do you feel at the end of the day? Most likely it was an empty feeling at best. The difference between doing something for the Lord and saying you're doing something for the Lord is huge, and the results are evident in how you feel when it's over.

> **Where in your life are you, even in the most subtle way, using God's name for personal gain instead of God's glory?**

Leader tip: Sometimes it feels like you're doing the right thing, but if you look at your motivation you see that the opportunity to profit personally, relationally, and financially far outweighs the possibility of profiting spiritually. Consider your church activities, your charitable works, your service opportunities, your business ventures, and your leisure activities. How many have the name of God associated with them? How many are really about furthering his kingdom, growing your relationship with him, or bringing glory to him?

> **How would your life be different if your motivation was solely to honor God instead of yourself? What would you need to change? What would the results look like?**

Leader tip: Consider a time when you did something for the pure motivation to serve, or to worship, or to honor God with your time, talents, and work. How did it feel? That is how it would feel to take all of the activities you are currently planning and make them somehow honor God as you complete them. That is the feeling you could live with every day. The feeling of fulfillment, that God is pleased with you and that you have done the right thing for the right reason, is one that you can claim every day.

■ CHAPTER 4: DON'T WORK YOUR LIFE AWAY

■ Where did you go on your last vacation?

Leader tip: The objective of this question is to create an easy environment to talk with one another about a focused topic. Focus on the more positive aspects of vacation—the relaxation, the chance to get to see new places, the time away from daily hassles and routines. You may want to save your story for last just in case you need it.

■ From the perspective of the father, the mother, and the boy, what might have each character been feeling during the flashbacks? What does the film say to you?

Leader tip: The father wouldn't slow down or take any time away from work to focus on his family. He was always going, and it had to impact him, the mom, and certainly the boy. Then it was too late. Have your group reflect on where in their lives they are like the father. Keep them focused and guard against tangents.

Read Genesis 1; 2:1–4. What did God do in each of the six days? What did he rest from on the seventh day?

Leader tip: Your group may want to debate whether Creation actually occurred in six literal days or if it is merely a figurative reference to time. Simply state that though those are valid differences of opinions, today's study is focused not on that greater issue but rather on the accomplishment of the work and the rest that followed. Further studies of Creation are something you can always choose to study later.

First Day:
He separated the dark from the light, creating night and day.

Second Day:
He separated the waters of the heavens and earth and called the space "sky."

Third Day:
He made the waters come together, leaving dry areas, and called them "sea" and "land." He produced all of the seed-bearing trees and vegetation on the land.

Fourth Day:
He made the solar system to govern the day and night; he placed the sun, moon, and stars in the sky.

Fifth Day:
He made all the fish and creatures in the sea and the birds of the air, commanding them to multiply. He created all fish and birds that create fish and birds of the same kind.

Sixth Day:
He made livestock, small animals, and wild animals—all animals that produce animals of the same kind.
He created human beings in his image to reign over all of the fish in the sea, the livestock, birds, wild animals, and small animals on the earth.
He created human beings as male and female and told them to multiply and fill the earth and govern over the animals and fish.

Seventh Day:
He rested from all of his work.
He blessed the seventh day and called it holy because he rested from all of his work.

■ What are some different ways in which people fill up their seven days each week?

Leader tip: We live in the busiest time in history. We do more because we have access to more. Before there were cars, a trip to the market could be most of what was accomplished in one day. Before the advancement in technology, getting one note or letter written and delivered could take days, but now it takes seconds and allows time for more and more opportunities and tasks to fill the day. It will create a lively discussion if you talk about why we are busier now than ever and then list specific tasks, opportunities, appointments, and activities that fill each day. Include driving distances, kids' activities, sports and physical fitness regimens, TV time, socializing, business meetings, travel, meaningful and meaningless time fillers.

■ What are all of the things you do in a typical week?

Leader tip: To answer this, you might want to have your group list out their activities for that specific day, and maybe the day before. And if they can, maybe even the day before that or look at what is on their calendar for tomorrow. Remind them to include mealtimes, sleeping, doctor's appointments, hair appointments, nail appointments, kid's sports, movies or TV time, work, driving time, pet time, cleaning, Bible studies, working in classrooms, volunteer work, and so on. It is also interesting to split the time into weekday and weekend times as tasks tend to vary drastically during those times.

Leader tip: Most people will be surprised by how much they actually do every day. The list can contain more than fifty activities per day, and with most people trying to sleep between six and eight hours a day, that leaves only sixteen to eighteen hours to accomplish those fifty-plus tasks. If you consider those things accomplished while "multitasking," it is truly incredible what can be achieved in one day. This is not an exercise to determine if the time fillers are worthwhile or not; it is merely an exercise to recognize how busy you are.

■ What would it look like to spend one out of every seven days either resting or taking a break from work?

Leader tip: Now take a minute to consider what would happen if one out of every seven days was dedicated to resting, taking a break from "all of the work" you do. What would happen to your physical and mental health? What would you "do" instead of all of the work?

The Sabbath can "just be a day of rest." How does this view of the Sabbath differ from your previous thoughts?

Note: People have a tendency to think of the Sabbath as a day for God. They think that if they are to observe the Sabbath, God is asking them to spend an entire day worshiping, contemplating him, and praying. God gave us the Sabbath for us; just as he took a full day of rest after creating the universe (something our busyness will never outdo), he has instructed us to take a day off from "all of the work."

CHAPTER 5: HONOR YOUR FATHER AND MOTHER

As a kid, what were some rules you had to obey that you thought were crazy or you just didn't like?

Leader tip: We all had rules that we thought were ridiculous when we were kids. Maybe it was the "clean everything on your plate before you can have dessert" rule. Or maybe it was the "be home before the streetlights come on" rule, which is crazy because how could you possibly know when they were going to come on until after they came on? Maybe you hated the rule that you had to make your bed every day when you knew you were just going to mess it up to sleep in it that night. There were many rules that made no sense when we were kids. Some of them do now, and some of them still seem crazy.

> **How is your family like / not like the family in the film?**
> **What makes honoring the grandmother easy? What makes it difficult?**

Leader tip: The first question can be one that begins to bring out some hard feelings and emotion in people's lives. It is important to be sensitive and not get sidetracked too early in the discussion. If people start talking about a difficult childhood, however, don't rush it or brush it off. Take time to let people feel listened to and cared for.

> **Read Ephesians 6:1–3 and Proverbs 23:22–25. What do you learn from these passages about the parent/child relationship?**

IMPORTANT leader tip: For this week's study, we will be dealing with the relationships between parents and children. For some in your group, this can be a very painful discussion, especially if there was abuse or if there is a fractured relationship. You may have someone in your group who was put up for adoption or who lived in the foster care system and never reconciled their feelings of abandonment and rejection. Even a good childhood can lead to hurt feelings and broken relationships due to decisions later in life. There may be estrangement issues as well. As a leader, be prepared to reassure those who are injured or hurt.

- Children should obey their parents because of their relationship to the Lord. • Children should obey their parents because it's the right thing to do. • They should honor their mother and father. • Honoring your parents brings the promise of things going well and a long life on earth. • Children should listen to their fathers. • Children should not despise their mothers. • Fathers of godly children know joy. • Give your father and mother joy by being godly.

■ What does *honor* mean? What doesn't it mean?

Leader tip: Honoring your father and mother is the use of respectful words and actions stemming from an inward attitude of esteem for their position. The original Hebrew word for *honor* means to "give weight to," much like you would weigh gold or money to find its value. But in this instance God means to make them weighty with respect, heavy with dignity and value through esteem. To honor them means to revere them and venerate them not for how they act or what they do, but instead because of who they are and their position as our parents.

Leader tip: Remind your group it is important to know the difference between honoring someone's position and honoring or condoning someone's behavior.

■ What are ways to honor parents at different stages of life (as a child, teenager, young adult, and adult, and as parents become elderly and pass away)?

Leader tip: Talk about what honor looks like at each stage of life. As a child, you would consider obedience and complete dependence. As a teenager, respect plays into the equation. Parents should be treated as having a position of authority. Have your group consider what is honoring to parents at each stage: the way people talk about their parents, including them in family functions, taking care of them as they grow older and require attention, how they talk about them after they're gone.

> **What are ways you've shown honor to your parents? How can you honor them at this point in your life? What about in the future?**

Leader tip: You might want to have your group get a pen and paper and make a list of ten things they would affirm in their parents. Even people who don't have great relationships with their parents can usually think of ten things they would affirm.

Leader tip: Think of the answers your group came up with. Which of those ways of honoring parents can your group embrace and show their own parents? Perhaps there are family traditions or practices of affirming one another that are meaningful to your own family that you can share with the group.

LIQUID would love to thank:

Chris Marcus, for being a producer, designer, editor, and director of photography on the project. You did it all, and we could not have done it without you.

Mariners Church: To the staff and small group department, for all of their help and insight into this entire project. And to the congregation and elder board for their prayers and support.

Kenton Beshore, for the beauty of flow questions.

All of the incredible people in North Carolina, who got this whole thing started.

The cast and crew, for the endless hours of hard work and incredible performances.

Aaron and Mark of Tank Creative, for making us sound good.

Chris Ferebee of Yates and Yates, for all of his guidance and direction.

Cindy Western, for her help in crafting great questions.

Pastor Bruce Nelson and the Mariners Church Stewardship Ministry, for all of their support and insight into the production of *The Ten: 1–5*.

Our incredible editor, Kim Hearon, who, to put it simply, had to deal with us. You made it fun.

All the people at Thomas Nelson, for your hard work and expertise.

And we thank God for having his hand on this project and blessing it.